Land Hermit Crabs

FROM THE EXPERTS AT
ADVANCED VIVARIUM SYSTEMS™

By Philippe de Vosjoli

THE HERPETOCULTURAL LIBRARY™
Advanced Vivarium Systems™
Laguna Hills, California

Karla Austin, *Director of Operations & Product Development*
Nick Clemente, *Special Consultant*
Jarelle S. Stein, *Editor*
Jill Dupont, *Production*
Kendra Strey, *Assistant Editor*
Cover and layout design by Michael Capozzi
Indexed by Rachael Rice

Cover photo by Andrew Lewis, courtesy of www.ihavecrabs.com.
The additional photographs in this book are by Andrew Lewis, courtesy of www.ihavecrabs.com., pp. 4, 6, 11, 12, 14, 15, 17,18, 19, 21, 23,
28, 31, 32, 36, 39, 41, 43, 46; Maleta and Jerry Walls, pp. 7–9, 26, 44,
51; Aaron Norman, pp. 48, 49, 52.

LCCN: 96-183295
ISBN-10: 1-882770-82-X
ISBN-13: 978-1-882770-82-3

An Imprint of BowTie Press®
A Division of BowTie, Inc.
23172 Plaza Pointe Dr., Ste. 230
Laguna Hills, CA 92653
www.avsbooks.com
866-888-5526

We want to hear from you. What books would you like to see in the
future? Please feel free to write us with any comments on our AVS
books.

Printed and bound in Singapore

12 11 10 09 08   5 6 7 8 9 10

CONTENTS

ACKNOWLEDGMENTS

This book would not have been possible without access to the scientific literature on land hermit crabs, especially *Biology of the Land Crabs* edited by Warren W. Burggren and Brian R. McMahon (Cambridge University Press, 1988), which proved to be an invaluable resource. The reader interested in knowing more about the biology of land hermit crabs should consult this important reference. I am also indebted to the various "crabbers" who have provided a wealth of information on hermit crab husbandry gathered from personal experience on their various Internet sites and forums. Any errors in the use or interpretation of scientific material are solely my own.

Hermit crabs' size and interesting behaviors makes them fun, appealing pets for both children and adults. Unfortunately, many beginning "crabbers" are unaware of the specific housing and care requirements these animals need to thrive.

INTRODUCTION

Land hermit crabs are one of the most widely kept of the land invertebrates. Their droll appearances and interesting behaviors have made them appealing to both children and adults looking for an affordable, low maintenance, and undemanding pet. Unfortunately, because hermit crabs are also considered cheap and disposable living toys, thousands die every year from neglect. At the root of the high mortality of captive hermit crabs is the failure to provide a proper environment. As with the keeping of tropical fish, the initial cost of a setup will be many times greater than the price of a hermit crab. Another reason for the high death rate of captive hermit crabs is simply a lack of knowledge about their requirements. Being arthropods, their way of life makes their care requirements significantly different from most popular pets such as hamsters, parakeets, or dogs and cats. For starters, land hermit crabs are tropical ectothermic (cold-blooded) creatures that depend on external heat to maintain a body temperature that allows them to be active. Because hermit crabs are arthropods, they don't have an internal skeleton but a hard exoskeleton that must be molted and replaced as they grow. Their growth occurs not continuously but in discrete stages associated with a molt cycle. Another unique feature of hermit crabs is their use of discarded snail shells. Although land hermit crabs have evolved to live away from seawater, they need to store water in the gastropod (snail) shell they carry. Providing the conditions to meet the requirements associated with these features is the key to successfully keeping land hermit crabs alive. The purpose of this book is to provide the essential information required for long-term maintenance of land hermit crabs as well as some useful information on their biology.

CHAPTER 1

GENERAL INFORMATION

Land hermit crabs are relatives of the often brightly colored marine hermits displayed in marine aquaria, but they spend most of their adult lives on the shore, venturing into shallow waters only to wet their gills and to breed. Like other hermit crabs, they are structurally somewhat between shrimp and true crabs, with the back legs reduced and the abdomen generally asymmetrical.

This typical hermit crab (*Coenobita clypeatus*) is also known as a Caribbean crab or purple pincher.

Taxonomy

Land hermit crabs are crustaceans in the family Coenobitidae, which includes all the land hermit crabs. The family consists of two genera, *Coenobita* with eleven species including the common land hermit crab of the pet trade, and the monotypic robber or coconut crab, *Birgus latro*, the largest land-dwelling crab. The land hermit crab commonly sold in the pet trade is the West Atlantic land hermit crab (*Coenobita clypeatus*). Besides land hermit crabs, there are species of intertidal hermit crabs in the family Diogenidae and several families of sea-dwelling hermit crabs.

Distribution

The West Atlantic land hermit crab that is commonly sold in the pet trade has a wide range in nature, from southern Florida and the Bahamas through the West Indies to Venezuela.

Size

West Atlantic hermit crabs grow to about 4 ounces (113 grams) body weight. Very old large specimens can weigh more than 7 ounces (200 g) and measure more than 6 inches (15 centimeters) long.

Note: From this point on West Atlantic land hermit crabs, which are the primary topic of this book, will be referred to as simply land hermit crabs or hermit crabs.

Anatomy

Crustaceans have a very different anatomy than mammalian vertebrates, and a special terminology is used to describe their anatomical parts. Hermit crabs have two main body segments: the cephalothorax, which is a fusion of the head and thorax (midsection); and the soft abdomen. In the land hermit crab, the soft abdomen twists to the right side to allow it to lodge itself within the empty shell of a gastropod (sea snail).

In the very front of the crab's body, you will notice two eyes connected to the body by eye stalks. Just below the eyes are two pairs of antennae—a pair of regular antennae and a

The fourth and fifth legs of a hermit crab are small and curved to help it hold on to the inside of its shell.

pair of antennules with bent tips. Beneath the two pairs of antennae are the mouthparts. Noteworthy are the elongated leg-like mouthparts called the third maxillipeds, used during eating and grooming of antennae.

A hermit crab has five pairs of legs, including a pair of large claws (which technically are called chelipeds or chelae) and four pairs of walking legs. The left claw is larger than the right claw and is used for defense and during locomotion. The smaller right claw is used during eating and drinking to transfer material to the mouth. The front two pairs of walking legs are kept outside the shell and used for walking. The back two pairs of walking legs are kept in the shell and used to anchor the crab inside its shell, perform grooming activities, and function in the course of reproduction.

Longevity

Most land hermit crabs die while in the aquatic larval stage. Only a small percentage of those that make it to land become breeding adults. It takes about two years for a land hermit crab to become a sexually mature adult. For a long, healthy life, a critical limiting factor is the availability of large suitable shells. Few large shells are available, and there is strong competition between large hermit crabs for these shells. Nonetheless, if food and large shells are available, a land hermit crab can continue to grow for many years, with giant specimens weighing up to 7 ounces (200 grams) and estimated to be at least thirty years old.

In captivity, most hermit crabs are dead within a year, mostly because they are not kept under the right conditions. However, a small percentage will live for several years; there are reports of some specimens living ten or more years in captivity.

Habits

The general pattern of larger hermit crabs is to rest in shelters, under litter, or partially burrowed during the day and to become active at night when the temperature is cooler and there are fewer predators. Smaller hermit crabs are commonly found close to shore where small shells are abundant. They may be active during the day.

This Caribbean hermit crab has discovered a potential new home in a larger shell and has crawled in to see if it's a good fit (top left). The crab then quickly uses its front legs to position the shell (top right), lifts its whole body over the shell opening (bottom left), and plops down into the shell. The whole prodcedure may take less than thirty seconds.

CHAPTER 2

SELECTION

Hermit crabs are now sold in many pet stores, gift shops, and stands along coastal boardwalks. Because hermit crabs often are sealed in their shells during the day, your opportunity for selection usually will be limited. Good general rules for selecting a healthy crab include the following.

- Avoid limp, sluggish hermit crabs that are partially or completely out of their shells and hang loosely when you pick them up. Healthy hermit crabs either withdraw into their shells or are out and active with antennae fluttering and claws ready to pinch. Sick hermit crabs can initially still be withdrawn in the shell but upon emergence are sluggish and demonstrate little fluttering of antennae.
- Select hermit crabs that feel heavy when picked up. Light hermit crabs may be dehydrated or sick.
- If there are many dead hermit crabs or crabs partially out of their shells, avoid buying a crab from that enclosure. It could be sick or seriously dehydrated.
- Some hermit crabs are missing limbs or the ends of limbs. Most of these will survive and regenerate their missing limbs after a few molts, but given the opportunity, select animals with a perfect appearance.
- Pick crabs that are active and vigorous, with fluttering antennae and quick withdrawal responses. Crabs that are feeding well are generally good choices.
- Inspect the crabs for mites, which appear as tiny light-colored arthropods seen crawling about the crab. Avoid mite-infested crabs.
- Size is a significant factor in selection. If you can afford only a small enclosure, you should purchase only small

crabs. The large ones need at least a 20-gallon (76-liter) tank. Large crabs are also messier and more destructive, so if you are interested in a nice display, smaller crabs are a better choice. Size is also a consideration if you want to handle your hermit crabs. For this purpose start off with small hermit crabs. They won't pinch as hard and won't be able to pinch as much skin. If you want larger hermit crabs, purchase sizeable ones to start with because hermit crabs simply do not grow that quickly.

How Many Hermit Crabs?

It is a good idea when possible to get more than one hermit crab. Aim for six small hermit crabs (1–1½ inches [2.5–3.7 cm]) per 10-gallon (38-L) setup, possibly more if you are buying very small specimens. You can keep up to four large land hermit crabs in a 20-gallon (76-L) tank.

If kept singly, a hermit crab will easily become lost in a large enclosure and will not be especially entertaining. You will be dependent on its level of activity for all opportunities of observation. If you have several hermit crabs, however, you'll be able to observe more hermit crabs involved in various activities. Some will climb and rest on wood, others may remain at ground level, and still others may burrow. In the evening, hermit crabs may gather in groups at a feeding dish and communicate by tapping their shells or stridulating (making noise by rubbing legs together). Simply said, a

It's best to keep several hermit crabs rather than a single crab pet. Keeping six or so crabs will allow you to better observe their natural behaviors and interactions.

small group of hermit crabs is a lot more fun to own than just one. In addition, observations in the wild indicate that hermit crabs are found in groups, and regular interactions are part of their lives. One of the benefits of living in groups is that it maintains a reservoir of shells allowing hermit crabs to exchange shells as they move up in size. While many West Atlantic land hermit crabs have lived long lives when kept singly, other species may fare best when kept in groups.

Cannibalism

Cannibalism has been reported in land hermit crabs. Large specimens may eat smaller ones. Hermits that have just molted are particularly vulnerable because of their soft exoskeleton, as are shell-less crabs that have been unable to find a suitable shell. To prevent cannibalism, you need only to:

- keep crabs together that are in the same size range;
- provide a burrowing medium for molting;
- make available a good selection of extra shells;
- and keep your hermit crabs fed well.

Personalities

Surprisingly enough, even creatures as primitive as hermit crabs will display variations in personality. Some will withdraw into their shells at the drop of a hat. Others will more readily emerge from their shells when picked up. Some pinch readily. Others are more reluctant to pinch their han-

C. perlatus gets its nickname, strawberry crab, because it resembles the bright red fruit of the same name.

dlers. You'll find some crabs are more lively and outgoing, while others are very secretive.

The Other Hermit Crabs

With the great popularity hermit crabs have achieved in recent years, new varieties have begun to appear on the market. The most widely available newcomer is the Pacific hermit crab (*C. compressus*), commonly offered as Ecuadorian hermit crabs, exotic hermit crabs, or as E-crabs. These are found along the western coast of the Americas from Mexico to Chile. They can be distinguished from the commonly sold West Atlantic land hermit crab by their elongated eyes, striping along the sides of the cephalothorax, and claws with the same general color of the body, versus the purple claws of West Atlantic hermits. Their habits are also slightly different. They tend to be more active and absolutely require a shallow container of seawater (use synthetic sea salts) in addition to freshwater. They also prefer a deeper substrate and need relatively constant warm temperatures in the mid 70s Fahrenheit.

Another species that is becoming more regularly imported from Indonesia is the bright red *C. perlatus*, sold under the name of strawberry hermit crab. Their requirements are similar to Ecuadorian hermit crabs.

Other species, such as *C. rugosus* and *C. brevimanus*, are also occasionally offered for sale. In general, their care will be similar to the above, with the common requirement for steady warmth, moderate to high relative humidity, and both freshwater and seawater.

Handling

The best way to pick up a hermit crab is to hold it by the back of the shell, keeping your fingers away from the claws. There is really no need to handle a hermit crab any other way. However, some owners decide they want to allow their hermit crabs to crawl on their hands. If you are one of those, my advice is to start with small hermit crabs, making sure you hold your hand flat. Do this over a table or a cushioned area. The problem with handling hermit crabs in this manner is that they can readily fall from a flat palm and injure themselves. Falls from several feet onto hard floor usually result in fatal injuries.

When you hold your crab, do so over a table or cushioned area. An unexpected pinch—especially from the claws of this large species, *C. brevimanus*—may startle you and cause you to accidentally drop the crab.

Another risk of free-handling a hermit crab is being seized by a claw and pinched. Some hermit crabs are ready pinchers. Others, if they feel as if they are falling or threatened, may hold onto skin with their claws. Hermit crabs have a very painful pinch. I have seen more than one child trying to maintain their composure as their pet hermit crab locked onto the skin between the thumb and index finger. With small crabs this hurts, but a larger hermit crab has more crushing power and will make you sweat with pain as you grit your teeth and try to remain cool. To get a hermit crab to release its grip, put it under running lukewarm water or dunk your hand into a container, such as a bucket or a sink, filled with lukewarm water and wait. Eventually the crab will let go.

Hermit crabs vary in their readiness to use their claws to pinch. Some owners claim that with handling, a hermit crab becomes less likely to pinch. If you really need an animal that can be handled with regularity, there are much better choices than hermit crabs.

CHAPTER 3
HOUSING

There are two basic ways to keep hermit crabs: the wrong way and the right way. For short life spans, hermit crabs are kept by what I call the prison approach. In a nutshell, this is keeping a hermit crab in a small plastic terrarium where it can barely move and where it usually will die after a few months. These crabs die because their small containers make it impossible to provide what they need. Besides being a death sentence, the prison approach makes it impossible for a hermit crab to behave normally because the container is too small. There is no room to climb or to burrow, and barely enough room for food and water. Obviously, I don't recommend this method.

The other method makes the assumption that no one knows better what a hermit crab needs than a hermit crab. It provides a variety of conditions from which a hermit crab is allowed to select what it wants. Because providing a variety of conditions (much as one finds in nature) requires space, at least a 10-gallon (38-L) and preferably a 20-gallon (76-L) all-glass aquarium will be required to keep small

For the more serious crabbers, there is no limit to the size of a crabitat. Shown here is a 100-gallon (379-L) model.

specimens. For larger hermit crabs, at least a 20-gallon tank and preferably a more spacious one will be required. Ideal enclosures are the all-glass reptile tanks with sliding screen tops. The tops prevent escape and allow you to rest sections of glass or Plexiglas on them to increase humidity and to add light fixtures if desired. If you must have a plastic terrarium, then buy the largest one you can afford. Recently, wire cages have been offered for keeping hermit crabs. These are unsuitable except in warm, humid areas of the United States such as Florida, and in warm, humid countries. If you decide to use wire caging you will have to include a container to hold burrowing-molting medium (see Burrowing-Molting Substrate section following).

Hermit crabs are best kept out of bedrooms unless you are a sound sleeper. They are active at night and can make quite a bit of noise such as tapping of the shells. Also avoid areas that may be subject to extremes of temperature. Most other areas will be suitable for hermit crabs, although placing an enclosure near an area where cleaning can easily be performed is generally a good idea. Spilling substrate on carpeting or carrying a heavy tank to another area of the house for cleaning may prove undesirable. Some people complain of the smell of commercial diets or moist foods. Food odors shouldn't be significant if you feed your hermit crab small amounts and daily remove uneaten food, but this could be a factor when considering placement of the enclosure. Finally, never place your tank in sunlight. It will become excessively hot and your crabs will overheat and die.

Escapes

Land hermit crabs are notorious escape artists. If there is any possible way to get out of an enclosure, they will usually find it. In an aquarium, any structure that can allow them to reach the top edge will be investigated, so you need to carefully consider the placement of landscape structures. If you are using an open-topped aquarium, make sure that wood and rock are in the center and not near the aquarium edges. As a general rule, it is a good idea to buy a screen cover for your hermit crab tank—it will help prevent any risk of escape, provide an area for you to place a light, and allow you to partially cover the top. Reptile enclosures include screen tops and are an easy way to fill this requirement.

Substrates

In the wild, land hermit crabs are found in areas ranging from close to the shoreline, which usually is sandy and littered with shells and broken coral, to inland where there is a layer of humus and leaf litter or soil on the ground. In captivity, hermit crabs will fare well on sand, sand-soil mixes, and aquarium gravel.

How Wet?

Hermit crabs are not rainforest creatures. They won't do well in soggy, wet enclosures. In the wild, the West Atlantic hermit crab usually is found in dry areas. The babies often are not too far from shore among shells, pieces of coral, and detritus that dry quickly in the sun. Larger hermits are usually found more inland, where there are trees, plants, driftwood, and sandy soil. The sun, breezes, and wind are all elements of the natural habitat that have drying effects. A good general rule is to keep the surface of your crab tank dry.

Sand

Most people select a fine grade (not powdery fine) sand because it is readily available in the pet trade and at large

Regularly rearrange your crabitat's landscaping so your crabs don't become bored in their enclosure.

hardware stores. Play-sand works well, as do the high-calcium sands now offered in the pet trade. Use at least 3 inches (7.5 cm) of sand for smaller crabs and up to 6 inches (15 cm) for large ones. Make a depression in a corner and pour in water slowly so that the bottom half of the sand layer is wet. There are two ways to provide water to your crabs in this kind of setup. Either you provide a shallow dish of freshwater or you can slope the sand so that a quarter of the tank has a depression you can pour water into. Simply add water to 50 percent of the height of the sand layer. As the water evaporates from the sand, it raises relative humidity. Hermit crabs also will be able to bury into the moist sand if they want to. In terms of ease of cleaning, a water dish is the better method of providing water. Sand is the preferred medium of most land hermit crab owners. Because it can become foul and smelly over time, regular replacement as needed is recommended.

As is common among most hermit crabs, this concave crab (*C. cavipes*) enjoys a sand substrate.

Coir Dust and Coir Dust–Sand Mixes

Coir dust is what remains after coconut husks are processed for fiber. It has a high water-holding capacity, offers excellent drainage and an acceptable pH, and even contains a certain amount of sodium that could be beneficial to hermit crabs. It is now sold as dry compressed bricks in pet stores, typically in the reptile supply section. Once soaked in water, these bricks will expand by up to eight times their volume. Many hobbyists have commented on how hermit crabs

Place food items into a dish rather than directly on the substrate to help keep debris off the food.

readily burrow into moist coir and how it makes an ideal molting substrate. Coir dust can also be mixed with sand, resulting in a substrate that could develop enough bioactivity that it could break down small amounts of waste. Bioactivity is best achieved in larger setups and with weekly stirring of the just moist (not soggy or wet) coir mix to move surface waste into the deeper bioactive layer.

Gravel

Gravel can be a functional and attractive substrate. You can pour a little water into the gravel layer to raise humidity. The problem with gravel is that it is not a good burrowing medium for hermit crabs that want to molt, so you need to include a plastic container (such as the type used for food storage) with a burrowing medium in your gravel bed setup (see Burrowing-Molting Substrate section below). When your tank gets too messy, gravel is easily washed clean. The plastic container with sand for burrowing can be easily removed to replace foul substrate. Gravel can be used successfully as a substrate for hermit crabs, but sand and sandy soil substrates are closer to what hermit crabs use in the wild.

Burrowing-Molting Substrate

No matter how you keep your hermit crabs, you need to maintain an area with a substrate that allows burrowing. The easiest way to do this is to add a wide and shallow flower pot or food storage container filled with either soil, moist coir dust, or a sand-soil or sand-coir mix. It should be slightly damp, not wet or soggy. Access to the container should be provided through a section of wood, cork bark, or rock. By providing this burrowing container you will allow hermit crabs to burrow when they want and offer suitable conditions for molting.

Landscaping Climbing Areas

Hermit crabs can be very active at night, and one of the things they like to do is climb. For this reason you should provide natural wood sections that are textured to permit easy climbing. Several kinds of wood are sold in the pet trade, including driftwood, grapevine, fig wood, and cholla cactus "skeletons." With the exception of driftwood, all of these woods should be kept on the dry land section or they will tend to mold and rot. One of the best landscape materials for hermit crab setups is cork bark, now regularly available by mail order or in the reptile supply section of pet stores. It is attractive, has a texture that allows for easy climbing, and can safely be eaten by hermit crabs. It also holds up very well when wet and is easily cleaned using a hose with a spray nozzle. It comes in various forms including hollow tubes, flat sheets, and curled pieces that can be stacked or positioned to form a range of structures, including shelters and areas under which hermits will bury prior to molting.

Caution

Remember to never use the wood of conifers (pine, redwood, cedar, etc.) in hermit crab setups. Their resins and the phenols they contain can be harmful to these crabs.

Shelters

In the wild, hermit crabs often will spend time in shelters or under logs, fallen leaves, and other detritus as well as inside tree hollows and depressions in rocks and burrows. Because relative humidity is higher in shelters and because shelters

A well-arranged cra-bitat should include plenty of structures for crabs to climb on. This setup uses rocks; tree branches also work well.

also provide protection from wind, they can help reduce evaporative water loss. A shelter also offers some protection from potential predators. Some land hermit crabs choose to molt in shelters instead of burrows. Cork bark is a light and attractive medium for creating a shelter, but other materials can be used, including oversized seashells, coconut shell halves with a wedge knocked out as an entrance, and PVC pipe sections partially buried in substrate.

Plants

If introduced in pots that are accessible to the crabs, plants eventually will be uprooted and dry out as a result of the crabs' burrowing activities. The crabs also may eat plants. To decorate your hermit crab tank with plants, place them in either pots that cannot be accessed or in glass jars of water with a foam cover. Good species for growing in water include arrowhead plants (*Syngonium*), pothos (*Epipremnum aureum*), and Chinese evergreens (*Aglaonema*). These are readily available in plant stores and houseplant sections of department stores.

Temperature, Heating, and Lighting

Land hermit crabs are found in subtropical and tropical areas. Because they are ectotherms (cold-blooded), they depend on the temperature of their environments to maintain body temperatures that allow them to be active. Besides lack of water, the most common cause of death in land hermit crabs is excessively cool temperatures. Thousands die during late fall, winter, and early spring when homes are maintained too cool for too long to meet hermit crabs' needs. If you have been to southern Florida during the winter, you have an idea of what the lower range of temperature tolerance is for land hermit crabs. In the wild, hermit crabs can seek shelter from bad weather by taking advantage of a variety of microhabitats, such as the inside of tree hollows and burrows and under decomposing vegetation, with temperatures that may be more favorable than the air temperature.

A temperature of 76°F–82°F (24°C–28°C) is ideal for high activity and feeding in hermit crabs. To maintain that range, most people will have to provide a heat source. Because a heating unit will take up a certain amount of space, it soon becomes clear why the small plastic terraria often sold as hermit crab homes are not suitable for keeping these creatures. The best way to heat a hermit crab tank is to use a subtank heating mat or heat tape. These heating units, sold in the reptile sections of pet stores, fit under a glass or plastic enclosure. (Be aware that heating pads designed for use with glass aquaria may melt plastic terraria; read all package instructions and warnings carefully.) If you plan on using such heating units, remember that they should cover no more than a third of the floor area so that crabs can get away from excess heat when they want. The other consideration is that you should use only a shallow layer of gravel, or preferably coir, when using this kind of heater. If you use a thick substrate layer, the heater will be relatively ineffective and there will be a risk of it cracking the bottom of the aquarium. Sand, because of its density, can form an insulating layer that will prevent heat from rising to the surface and will cause it to build up at the glass level. This can make the bottom glass pane of the aquarium expand to the degree that it may crack.

Another widely used heating source for hermit crabs is incandescent light bulbs. They should be placed in a reflector-type fixture over a screen-covered all-glass enclosure. The red incandescent bulbs sold for reptiles are a better choice than regular white incandescent bulbs during cool months because

Since hermit crabs are nocturnal, a moon-simulating light makes for wonderful night viewing.

they can be kept on all night. For smaller tanks of 5 to 10 gallons (19 to 38 L), incandescent aquarium strip reflectors will also work well. In the larger size tanks, standard elongated incandescent aquarium bulbs may not generate enough heat. If you have a tank of 29 gallons (110 L) or larger, an economical alternative is to use a ceramic heat emitter as sold in the reptile section of pet stores. When using incandescent bulbs or ceramic heat emitters over hermit crabs, selecting the right wattage will be critical to prevent overheating. Only a thermometer will allow you to accurately determine temperatures in your setup. Incandescent bulbs and heat emitters cannot be used with most plastic terraria because of the danger of melting the plastic.

At low temperatures, 74°F (23°C) and below, hermit crabs will become less active and feed little, if at all. They can survive cool temperatures in the 60s F for brief periods of time, but if kept long-term at suboptimal temperatures, they will eventually die. Remember, a temperature of 76°F–82°F (24°F–28°C) is ideal for land hermit crabs.

Temperature Controllers

The reptile heat mats and heat tapes commonly used to heat hermit crab enclosures can produce surface temperatures from around 90°F (32°C) to just higher than 100°F (38°C). One way to achieve the desirable range for hermit crabs is to buy a smaller size mat than what is recommended for the size setup you have; for example, use the size for a 10-gallon (38-L) rather than one recommended for your 20-gallon (76-L) tank. Still, this will not assure you have the proper temperature range for your crab setup. The heat output of subtank heaters and ceramic heat emitters can be controlled by plugging them into a rheostat time controller (e.g., a light or fan dimmer capable of handling the wattage of a heater) and with the help of a thermometer adjust their output until the right temperature range is achieved. It's even better to buy an on/off thermostat with an external probe (sold in reptile supply sections of pet stores) and simply set it to the desired temperature.

Thermometers

There is only one way to know what the temperature is in your hermit crab tank, and that is to use a thermometer. Several kinds are now sold in the pet trade, ranging from inexpensive stick-on types to dial and glass thermometers. You can also buy digital thermometers with an external probe or sensor in some department stores and electronic supply stores. Place the thermometer body at the cooler side of the tank and the probe on the heated side. The inside setting will inform you of the air temperature and the outside setting will give you a read-out of the area with the external probe.

Lighting

Because most hermit crabs spend the day concealed in some kind of shelter, no additional lighting should be required to keep your hermit crabs healthy. However, there are anecdotal reports that hermit crabs may benefit from brief weekly exposure to the sun or to high-output UVB fluorescent reptile bulbs. The value of a UVA or UVB light source as a tool for successfully keeping hermit crabs needs to be further investigated. If you decide to expose your crabs to sunlight, place them in an aluminum screen cage or in a fine wire-mesh cage. Do not place glass-sided or plastic hermit crab enclosures in the sun. The cages will overheat and the hermit crabs will die.

CHAPTER 4

WATER

Hermit crabs, like most animals, require water to survive. Failure to provide water is probably the most common cause of death in captive animals. Although the hermit crab is no longer adapted to living in water, it does need to carry water wherever it goes. Water is stored in the borrowed gastropod (snail) shell it calls home. The tight sealing abdominal portion of the crab plays a key role in sealing in shell water. Shell water is maintained by dipping into a body of water or by drinking. To drink, a land hermit crab transfers water to the mouth using its small claw. Water that is ingested through drinking can be drawn into the branchial (gill) chambers and expelled into the shell.

Hermit crabs, however, do not depend exclusively on the availability of water from a dish. They also obtain water from food such as vegetation, fruit, and the flesh of other animals. Because they also tend to store fat, they probably can obtain metabolic water from the breakdown of fat. There also is speculation that water may be obtained from moist substrates.

Generally, West Atlantic hermit crabs fare best on freshwater or brackish water (up to 50 percent the salinity of oceanic seawater) but usually will not fare well long-term if given exclusively full-strength seawater. In captivity, they should be given both dechlorinated (buy dechlorinator/dechloraminator drops at a pet store or use bottled drinking water) high-quality freshwater and brackish water (five tablespoons of rock salt or seawater mix per gallon [3.8 L] of water) in separate shallow dishes, such as the reptile food and water dishes now sold in the pet trade.

Do not use deep dishes with smooth sides. In deep containers, the crabs will have difficulty accessing the water and

The large, purple claw serves as an operculum to seal water in the shell during dry conditions.

may drown if they fall into the dish. A good water level is about half the height of the crab when at rest in its shell. In deeper dishes or containers, place rocks in the water to allow the crabs to climb out easily. The water should be changed every one to two days or whenever fouled. It is important that you monitor the water level to make sure that water is available at all times. Too often I see pet stores display hermit crabs on dry substrate with no water. That is a primary reason why many pet stores lose large numbers of hermit crabs.

High Quality Water

It cannot be emphasized enough that you should not use tap water treated with chlorine or chloramines for hermit crabs without first dechlorinating/dechloraminating with a dechlorinator/dechloraminator sold in the aquarium sections of pet stores.

Why Brackish Water?

Many books for good reasons recommend that only freshwater be offered to hermit crabs. They will in fact do fine with freshwater, as long as they have a source of salts in their diet or environment. Remember that the water in the shell is maintained at a certain ion concentration that is adjusted through behaviors, drinking of water, and ingestion of salts. Given a choice of both fresh and brackish waters, a hermit crab will select what it feels it needs for proper hydration.

The normal course is for hermit crabs to select freshwater, but after acquiring a new shell a hermit crab may initially select brackish water to maintain the proper ion concentration in the stored water of the new shell. Because we cannot control ion and water balance in hermit crabs, the best course is to provide conditions that allow them to select what they prefer. I recommend providing two types of water, fresh and brackish, in separate dishes.

Water pH and Hardness

I add crushed coral to the water area to increase water hardness and raise pH. In a sloped tank I edge the water section with crushed coral sold for marine aquaria. I also recommend placing a small amount of crushed coral in water dishes. Other hermit crab owners have recommended that cuttlefish bone or a seashell be placed in the water.

Misting

In nature, hermit crabs tend to be particularly active following rains. For this reason it is recommended that they be lightly misted on a daily basis in the early evening. To prevent the accumulation of mineral stains on the walls of the enclosure, use purified water (available bottled at supermarkets and drug stores) when misting. Misting will provide water for drinking and help raise the relative humidity.

Daily Dipping

Many books recommend daily dipping of hermit crabs into water. This is done to ensure that a hermit crab gets enough water and keeps its gills wet. This may be especially valuable for newly purchased hermit crabs because many are dehydrated. However, this should not be necessary if you keep your crabs in a well-designed setup. The secret to a land hermit crab being able to survive away from water is that it carries water within its shell. For its gills to function properly, the necessary water is obtained from that stored within the shell. When a hermit crab backs into its shell, the volume of the abdomen displaces stored water, causing it to rise and bathe the gills. A healthy crab doesn't need daily dipping.

However, a hermit crab does more than just carry water; it also regulates the concentration of salts in shell water. By dipping a crab in freshwater you are assuming that you know better than the crab how much freshwater it needs and that you also know better the best course of action to maintain ion concentrations in the shell water. If kept in the right kind of setup, daily dipping of crabs is unnecessary.

Active bathing—by dipping it into dechlorinated water—should clean off any body debris. Bath water must be lukewarm; water that is too warm or too cold will stress your crab.

Relative Humidity

Relative humidity is a measure of how much water is contained in air as water vapor; it is measured by a device called a hygrometer. Generally, hermit crabs do best at 78 to 90 percent relative humidity. One of the effects of high relative humidity is that it reduces the rate at which evaporative water is lost. As temperatures drop in the evening, some of the water in the air may condense and provide a source of water. In short, a hermit crab will be able to conserve water and will be less likely to dehydrate in a high humidity environment. Anyone who has been to southern Florida or the Caribbean knows the high humidity of the hermit crab's native habitat.

The first step to raising relative humidity is to create an evaporative water source. If you use a deep substrate, keeping the bottom layer moist will provide an area from which water will be able to evaporate. If you have a shallow, dry substrate, you can introduce a sponge humidifier to increase air humidity. This is simply a piece of polyurethane foam or sponge placed in a shallow container of water. The high surface area of the foam allows water to evaporate at a good rate. A popular alternative is to use natural sponge. Remember to regularly wash sponges in pure water (no soap) to remove scum and reduce bacterial colonization. A very effective way to raise the relative humidity is to mist the tank nightly, using purified water to prevent the accumulation of mineral stains on the glass. As the water evaporates, the air humidity rises.

To stabilize humidity in your hermit crab tank, you also should cover the half of the tank's top that is not occupied by a heat light. A piece of Plexiglas cut to size works well as a tank cover. As a quick and temporary measure you can use a piece of clear plastic wrap, being careful not to place it beneath the light source.

Ventilation

Notice that I only recommend covering part of the top of the enclosure. Hermit crabs usually will not do well in sealed wet environments such as a closed terrarium. Wind or breeze and a dry substrate surface are features of their natural habitats. A sealed environment also will speed the growth of molds and bacteria in the tank. Allow for air flow.

CHAPTER 5

FEEDING

H ermit crabs are opportunistic, scavenging omnivores that can eat a wide range of foods, from fruit and vegetation to insects, carrion, and even feces. They have a good sense of smell and are capable of locating food several feet away by using olfactory cues. Foods with strong smells, such as ripe fruit or a dead animal, are recognized readily.

In captivity, food should be offered in shallow dishes to prevent rapid fouling of the tank. Hermit crabs aren't the neatest eaters in the world, so you will need to perform an occasional tank cleanup. Hermit crabs, if one studies their anatomy, have a small gut. This means that they will eat very small amounts per feeding session. For this reason you only need to offer small portions of food when feeding these crabs. Excess food will simply go to waste and end up rotting and smelling up whatever room the crabs are kept in.

There now are several commercial hermit crab diets that will form a good base diet for your animals. However, all hermit crab foods are not created equal. Some commercial diets will not be liked by your crab. Other diets, even if eaten by your crabs, may stink and be intolerable to you, while yet others will be relished and acceptable to both crab and man. If your hermit crab does not like one brand of hermit crab food, then try another. Tropical fish flakes and fish foods are good alternatives to hermit crab diets, as are moistened dog kibble and pieces of fish or shrimp with the shell on. Hermit crabs also will eat dead insects including the freeze-dried flies and crickets now sold in the reptile sections of pet stores. Prekilled mealworms and crickets coated with calcium supplement can be offered for variety. Hermit crabs also feed on plant matter, including romaine lettuce (which has a good level of calcium) and fruit such as grapes (one of

This hermit crab enjoys a banana. Other favorite fruits include grapes, papayas, and peaches.

their favorites), apples, bananas, and papayas. Hermit crabs also enjoy dried fruit and have a particular preference for dates and raisins.

Diet and Color

As with many other crustaceans, the bright color of hermit crabs is derived from the ingestion of certain carotenoid pigments. Indeed, the color of most land hermit crab species will fade, notably the bright reds of strawberry hermit crabs and the yellows and oranges of Ecuadorians, unless they are offered a source of these pigments. Although feeding plant matter rich in carotenes is often recommended by crab hobbyists, no research has been done to show how effectively such pigments are used by hermit crabs to intensify reds and oranges. The most effective pigment for this purpose is astaxanthin, which is primarily obtained from algae, notably microalgae such as *Haematococcus pluvialis*; the best sources are color-enhancing fish flakes (read the label), plankton, and other crustaceans, such as krill and whole small shrimp. However, fruits and vegetables rich in other carotenes should be regularly offered because they also may contribute to exoskeleton color. We do know that diet does influence color and that other ingested compounds, such as tannins of various tree leaves and bark, can alter the appearances of hermit crabs, for example by making them darker or more brown.

Brightly colored species, such as this strawberry crab, benefit from carotene-rich foods such as cooked carrots to help maintain the crabs' rich colors.

Natural sources of carotenes include apricot, papaya, peach, collard greens, cooked carrot, cooked sweet potato, and cooked squash.

Treats

Hermit crabs like fatty foods as well as foods with a nutty odor. These should be offered in moderation as part of a varied diet. Two of their favorites are raw coconut and peanut butter. When I was looking for various land hermit crabs on the small islands of New Caledonia, I would put sections of open coconut on stakes along various trails during the day. At night, swarms of hermit crabs, including the occasional coconut crab, gathered to feed on the

This jumbo-sized hermit crab enjoys nibbling on raw coconut.

coconut. I also experimented with gobs of peanut butter and had even greater success.

Popcorn is another hermit crab favorite. Place a few popped kernels in your tank at night and watch your hermits come to life. Other treats that may be beneficial for hermit crabs include salty foods such as crackers—some crabbers report their hermits are particularly fond of cheese-flavored varieties.

Supplements

Little is known of the nutritional requirements of hermit crabs, but by feeding them a varied diet, most of their required nutrients will be provided. The one supplement that I recommend is calcium in the form of powdered calcium carbonate such as crushed oyster shell and cuttlefish bone.

Maintenance Schedules

Keeping hermit crabs healthy requires regular maintenance schedules.

Regular Maintenance

- Check your hermit crabs without removing animals from shelters or burrows.
- Provide small amounts of food and clean water. The food and water containers should be washed when dirty either by running through a dishwasher or using an antibacterial dish detergent and *thoroughly* rinsing before use. After running through a dishwasher or using a dish detergent, soak the containers in water for twenty-four hours prior to use; rinse again to remove any detergent residue. Some specialists recommend cleaning containers only by thoroughly wiping their sides using paper towels rather than resorting to a detergent, which could possibly kill crabs if not thoroughly rinsed off.
- Scattered food debris should be removed as well as fecal material observed on the substrate surface.
- Mist your crabs at least once in the early evening.

Monthly Tasks or As-Needed

- Replace substrate.
- Replace damaged or dead plants.
- Replace or clean landscape materials as needed. If a 5 percent bleach solution is used as a disinfectant to clean landscape materials, allow them to sit overnight in a container of clean water after rinsing to remove all traces of bleach and detergent.
- Clean sides of tank.

Did You Know?

Hermit crabs excrete urine through their antennal glands, located at the bases of the antennae.

CHAPTER 6

MOLTING

Like other crustaceans such as shrimp and lobsters, hermit crabs molt (shed their integument or exoskeleton) on a regular basis as they grow. During a molt cycle, four stages occur. During the first stage (proecdysis or premolt), the new integument is formed beneath the old one, water is absorbed in the body, and calcium as well as other nutrients are absorbed from the exoskeleton. The second stage (ecdysis or molt) is the actual molting process. The old integument is shed off and the crab increases its size by absorbing water. Right after a molt, a hermit crab will appear pink and will be very soft and vulnerable. The third stage (postmolt) allows the new integument to harden into an exoskeleton. Stored calcium and nutrients are mobilized, the old shell is eaten, and food and water are ingested to supply lost calcium and the nutrients necessary for the new larger body. The new exoskeleton hardens. The end result is a slightly larger crab that eventually will have to hunt for a new larger shell. The fourth stage of the molting cycle is the period between molts and is called the intermolt period. In the wild, adult hermit crabs molt once a year. In captivity, several factors affect the molt cycle, including steady availability of food.

The hermit crab remains in the shell during most of the molt. Both in the wild and in captivity, hermit crabs select secure places to molt such as natural shelters under fallen wood or litter or in burrows excavated in the substrate. They may remain in burrows for up to two weeks before molting. A hermit crab will remain in its shell during most of the molt. Following molting, a hermit crab increases its body volume by absorbing water. Because a great deal of body calcium is lost during the molting process, a hermit crab will consume its molted exoskeleton to quickly regain some of

the lost calcium. Thus, you should not remove the skin of a crab that has just molted.

Preventing Molt-Related Deaths

In general, molting is a vulnerable period for hermit crabs. A small percentage of hermit crabs both in the wild and in captivity die during the molting process. One of the great difficulties in keeping the coconut crab, which is the largest of the hermit crabs, is providing the conditions that allow molting. For this giant species, a substrate depth of about 2 feet (61 cm) will be required. In captivity, the risk of hermit crabs dying during molting is high because of the following five factors.

- Not enough water has been provided. As mentioned before, dehydration probably is the most common cause of death of hermit crabs in captivity.
- Excessive handling. Owners are concerned when they see their crab hidden and inactive for several days, and they feel compelled to dig it out of its molting refuge and handle it. Handling a hermit crab during molting can cause fatal harm.
- The exoskeleton, an important source of calcium, is removed following molting.
- No shelter or refuge is provided. Hermit crabs like to dig in soft substrate such as a soil-sand mix when molting or seek access to a shelter.

- Cannibalism. A hermit crab that is kept with other crabs that aren't fed adequately or are much larger, is housed with inadequate shelter, or is injured in the molting process may be cannibalized.

Molting Schedules

Small, immature hermit crabs will molt several times a year, but as they grow older and larger they may molt only every twelve to eighteen months depending on various conditions such as temperature, diet, and injury. Prior to molting, a land hermit crab will hide in a burrow or shelter for about two weeks. Once the old exoskeleton has been cast, a hermit crab has a pale body color and will be very soft and vulnerable to both predators and contact injuries (do not handle it). If by chance you find your hermit crab pale and soft with the old exoskeleton next to it, cover the crab with a shelter without disturbing it. Over the next seven to ten days following molting, a hermit crab will eat its molted exoskeleton and regain some of the calcium required for its new exoskeleton to harden. When all is said and done, you're looking at three to four weeks for a molt cycle to be completed.

Regeneration of Lost Limbs

The life of a crab is hazardous, and loss of or damage to limbs, claws, or antennae may occur. Like other crabs, hermit crabs have the ability to, over a period of several molts, regenerate a leg or limb sections severed at a joint.

CHAPTER 7

BREEDING AND OTHER BEHAVIORS

ermit crabs have become the most widely-kept of invertebrates largely because of their interesting behaviors. These palm-sized pets' twitching antennae and constant shell-swapping—among other activities—provide endless entertainment for crabbers. Increasing interest in designer shell design also has helped boost crab-keeping popularity.

Breeding

Because of the difficulty of rearing newly hatched hermit crabs, these neat animals usually are not bred in captivity. It is simply easier to manage wild populations of hermit crabs. Nonetheless, the breeding pattern of hermit crabs is worth knowing about because it will give you insights into the reproduction of crustaceans.

Mating usually occurs near the shoreline, when large numbers of land hermit crabs migrate toward the shore for breeding. During mating, both crabs extend partially out of the shell and copulation occurs ventral surface to ventral surface (belly to belly) with the male passing a spermatophore to the female.

Following mating and later fertilization, the eggs, which may number up to 50,000, are released by females along the shoreline. After the eggs hatch, newborn hermit crabs start off as tiny sea-dwelling planktonic larvae called zoeae. This planktonic stage lasts about a month. In the next stage, the tiny hermit crabs are aquatic but already seek tiny shells as their homes. They then reach land and eventually transfer to shells on the shore. Once established on land, it requires about two years for baby land hermit crabs to become sexually mature adults.

Shell-Changing

From the time they are land-dwelling, hermit crabs depend on a shell to provide protection and to store water. Finding the right shell is critical to survival, and only the hermit crab can determine if a shell has the right fit. Shells preferred by West Atlantic hermit crabs form concentric spiral coils. They are broad on the outside and become narrower as they coil toward the center. The opening of the shell is more or less round. A good shell will allow a hermit crab to withdraw into it and effectively seal access to vulnerable body parts with the crab's large claw and second walking leg. Water-holding capacity, snugness, weight, and drag when moving probably are all factors in the selection of what a hermit crab eventually considers a good home.

Generally, the opening of the shell should be slightly larger than the large claw, but other factors such as shell structure will be considered by the hermit crab. Besides providing a shelter, the home shell also is an important water storage structure. Finding a shell that can be well-sealed by the abdomen to hold stored water is critical to the welfare of a hermit crab. For West Atlantic hermit crabs, spiral coiling, broadly conical seashells appear to be the best choices. In the

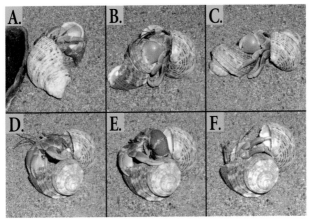

Sizing up a prospective new home (A), this hermit crab rolls the new shell over to dump out any foreign materials (B). The crab then positions the new shell to facilitate the swap (C). It climbs out of the old shell (D) and slips into the new shell (E). The crab decides the new shell is a good fit (F).

pet trade, turbo shells and murex are the most commonly sold shells for hermit crabs. The shells of land snails and tree snails will also work for smaller specimens. Shells can be bought either from businesses that specialize in hermit crabs or from shell shops. You should offer several extra shells, including some that are about the same size and others that are somewhat larger than the one in which your hermit crab currently lives. As your hermit crab grows, it will require increasingly larger shells to call home.

Note that Ecuadorian hermit crabs require shells with a wider, more oval opening than West Atlantic land hermit crabs. Providing the right shells will require some effort (they use *Nerita* shells, also called nerites, in parts of their range; these are sold by shell dealers) and is best accomplished by offering a selection of broad, spiraling shells with a width slightly larger than the cephalothorax. Dealers that specialize in hermit crab shells offer *Nerita, Babylonia,* and *Phasianella* shells with broader openings that will be adopted by this species.

A good shell is critically important to hermit crabs, and they will spend time investigating other shells, trying them out and so on. Empty shells, for good reasons, are fascinating to hermit crabs.

Cleaning Shells

It is a good idea to disinfect new shells or shells previously used by hermit crabs by boiling them in water for about fifteen minutes. Let them cool and empty the water from shells before introducing them into the tank.

Fancy Shells

The external appearance of a shell is of minor importance to a hermit crab but often is important to owners. In fact, it commonly is the main reason a hermit crab is purchased in the first place. There now are many select, ornamental, hand-painted shells sold for hermit crabs in the pet trade. A concern is that the shells are painted with safe materials (usually acrylic paints) and properly sealed, but it appears that most suppliers have addressed this issue. The paint

This Caribbean hermit crab chose a rainbow-colored shell for its current home. Shell designing has become quite popular among crabbers. Themes range from simple color patterns to detailed displays such as sports team logos and cartoon characters. Designer shells can be purchased, or you can paint them yourself.

eventually will chip off to some degree, and it is possible that this could harm hermit crabs, but I could not find any clear evidence for this claim. You should, however, make sure that only the outside of the shell is painted, never the inside. Also, do not boil painted shells prior to use; the paint or sealer will soften, become sticky, and peel off.

Hermit crabs and their shells are a form of living art in progress, and we can expect further development of this area, including new safe media and changes in trends. For the purists, the better course is to shop shell stores and buy the most colorful natural shells you can find.

Only the outsides of shells should be painted. Paint on the shells' insides potentially could chip off and be ingested by the crab.

Shell-less

In the wild, hermit crabs out of their shells are vulnerable to dehydration and predators. They will not survive long when shell-less. The same is true in captivity, which is why it's critical that you make available a variety of shells for your crab. Whenever a hermit crab finds a new shell, the animal must condition it to fit its needs. This means grooming parts of the shell and accumulating a water reservoir with the proper ion concentration. Hermit crabs sometimes leave an old shell, try a new shell, decide the new shell is not so great after all, and go back to the former shell. The search for the perfect shell is one of the hermit crab's continuing endeavors in life. Because in nature large shells are less common than small shells, one of the problems that larger hermit crabs encounter is the inability to find shells large enough to accommodate them. That is one reason why very large hermit crabs are relatively uncommon.

Complex Behaviors

If you watch your hermit crab carefully, you can notice that it has a variety of different and interesting behaviors. The crab doesn't think as such, but it reacts in predictable (stylized) ways to certain actions by other crabs or predators, and to the environment.

Sound Production

Anyone who has kept hermit crabs will tell you they're noisy little critters. If kept in a bedroom they can keep you awake with their clanging around as they climb or bang against glass and shuffle among shells.

Land hermit crabs also produce clicking sounds by intentionally tapping the shells and rapping legs as well as make stridulating sounds by rubbing legs together. This noise-making is used in hermit crab communication, including aggressive displays. If a hermit crab tries to climb onto another or makes contact with it, both crabs may stridulate in annoyance.

Defense

The normal defensive response of a hermit crab is to withdraw into its shell and seal the opening with the enlarged left claw and third walking leg. They will perform this withdrawal response in reaction to perceived movements by large moving objects (potential predators). In the wild, you can see this behavior close to shore where babies may suddenly back into their shells and roll a little way if they are on a slope. Hermit crabs in trees also will withdraw into their shells when they feel threatened, often causing them to fall to the ground. When picked up, some hermit crabs withdraw, while others may emerge from their shells ready to move or, if necessary, pinch what they can grab.

Autotomy

If threatened, hermit crabs can cast off a limb. Hypothetically, this can hold the attention of a predator as the crab scuttles away. In captivity, autotomy often is witnessed with dying crabs. They will drop a claw or leg more readily than will a healthy crab and will sometimes do so for no apparent cause.

Antennal Activity

Hermit crabs are not the most expressive animals in the world, but their levels of activity can give you an indication

of what motivates and excites them. In general, when in the presence of food or when following olfactory cues, they will display a high level of antennal activity, dipping the antennae down and up.

Grooming

Land hermit crabs perform various grooming behaviors including keeping the eye stalks and the antennae free of dirt and debris. Specialized brushlike structures (setae) on mouthparts (third maxilliped) are used to groom the antennae and eye stalks. The various legs also groom each other to various degrees. The back legs are used to groom the shell and its edges.

Defecation

A question sometimes asked by puzzled keepers concerns hermit crab defecation. Do they defecate in the shell? No, they do not defecate in their shells; they curve their abdomens so as to defecate out of the shell. Fecal matter can sometimes be seen on the substrate surface in the form of thin fecal strings.

CHAPTER 8

DISEASES AND PROBLEMS

Like most organisms, hermit crabs are subject to a variety of problems ranging from nutritional disorders to parasites and various infections. However, little work has been done on identifying the early stages of diseases and the most effective treatments. Generally, the best procedure is to prevent problems by providing good care for your hermit crab.

Signs of Illness

There are two common signs of illness in a hermit crab—sluggishness and little or no movement of antennae. A dying hermit crab doesn't have the energy to behave normally. It barely has the strength to anchor into its shell and may even have dragged itself out of the shell. In virtually all cases, if your basic husbandry is correct, then there will be little you can do to save the poor hermit crab. Even in cases where poor husbandry, such as dehydration, may be a factor, damage to the crab from lack of water often will be beyond repair.

Problems Related to Husbandry

Providing a hermit crab with its basic requirements is essential to prevent serious problems. Following are seven reminders to help ensure your hermit crabs thrive.

- Temperature. Hermit crabs are subtropical to tropical creatures. It is common for hermit crabs to die during the cold winter months when not enough heat is provided. Conversely, hermit crabs will die if a tank is overheated.

This healthy hermit crab sits atop a rock in its crabitat. Crabs need plenty of structures to climb on to stay active and healthy. Decreased activity level is an early sign that your crab may be ill.

- Hydration. I see hermit crabs in pet shops displayed with no water so often that it is safe to say that many members of the public also neglect water when caring for their hermit crabs. Dehydrated hermit crabs initially will choose to tightly withdraw within the shell to reduce water loss, but later, even if dipped in water, may be too damaged to recover. A sign that a crab is dehydrated is that it will emerge and spend long periods in water when placed in it but will be relatively sluggish with little or no fluttering of antennae. The likelihood for these crabs recovering is poor. This is one of the most common causes of death in hermit crabs. Use a routine for maintenance of your animals, misting them nightly and providing them with an easily accessible water dish.
- Relative humidity. This is a vital part of providing hermit crabs with enough water. Humidity should be 70 to 90 percent, but the substrate surface of your crab tank should be relatively dry and certainly not soggy.
- Burrowing. Failure to provide a burrowing medium for molting is a common cause of death. Land hermit crabs need a place to burrow.
- Diet. Hermit crabs have definite nutritional requirements, including a need for dietary calcium. Feed them a varied and high-quality diet. Making salt available in the form of brackish water is recommended.

- Cleanliness. Keeping the enclosure clean and regularly providing fresh water and food in clean containers is important for the long-term health of your hermit crab.
- Certain aerosol sprays, such as hair sprays and household cleaners, can have a harmful effect on hermit crabs. Do not keep crabs in areas where such sprays are used.

Parasites

In the wild, hermit crabs are parasitized by flies and mites. In captivity, mites are sometimes found on hermit crabs. Because many miticides are potentially toxic to hermit crabs, getting rid of mites is difficult. Crabs can be dipped in seawater or mites can be removed individually by applying a section of rolled Scotch tape to the mite. Generally any infestation of mites will require procedures to prevent their spread and reinfection. This means keeping crabs in simply designed enclosures that are cleaned regularly with all materials replaced on a regular basis.

Little is known of the other diseases of hermit crabs and even less about how to treat them. Some owners, when hermit crabs appear sluggish and ill, use a "shotgun approach," dipping them once or twice daily in antibiotic solutions used for treating fish. The effectiveness of these treatments has yet to be determined.

CHAPTER 9

OTHER CRABS FOR FRESHWATER AQUARIA

There are many families of crabs living in the oceans of the world, but relatively few occur on land even on tropical islands. In addition to land hermit crabs, a few terrestrial or intertidal crabs are occasionally sold as pets.

Fiddler Crabs

Fiddler crabs (*Uca* spp.) usually are displayed in pet stores in aquatic freshwater tanks with no access to land. Several species are now offered, and the basic characteristics for care are the same. Males have an enlarged claw, usually white, while females have two diminutive claws. Fiddler crabs will survive only a few weeks under the conditions used by most stores for display. They should be maintained in setups where crabs have access to a land area with rocks or wood.

The large, white claw tells you that this fiddler crab is male.

Instead of the large claw as seen in male fiddlers, females have two small claws.

They need some salt in the water. There are reports of individuals kept alive for a year or more in water with only one to two tablespoons of rock salt or seawater mix per gallon (3.8 L). In the wild, fiddler crabs live in areas with seawater or brackish water. They molt in water. The biggest problem with fiddler crabs is provision of an adequate diet. Fiddler crabs are deposit feeders and incapable of breaking up chunks of food for ingestion. The best technique is to have a substrate of sand or fine aquarium gravel and offer powdered flake food. The crabs will process fine sand through their mouths and sift out biological material.

Red-Clawed Freshwater Crabs

These small Asian crabs, commonly identified as *Sesarma bidens*, usually are displayed in aquaria with no access to land, and they typically are dead within a few weeks. I have housed them in a sloped sand setup with a section of water in a tank with small hermit crabs. Interestingly, these crabs spend a great deal of time on land, thus they should be kept in shoreline vivaria. They enjoy dead crickets and fish flakes. They are best kept in a setup dedicated to only them because they are vulnerable to predation following a molt. Nonetheless, in a large enough setup that is not too crowded, they can be kept with small hermit crabs; their high level of activity can enliven a hermit crab setup.

Coconut Crabs

Very rarely, live young specimens of the coconut crab, *Birgus latro*, also known as the robber crab, are imported into the United States and offered by reptile dealers. There are two forms—the red coconut crab and the black coconut crab. Red specimens, such as some of the ones from Aldabra, are a brilliant orange-red. Coconut crabs are impressive and can make quite a display in public zoos and aquaria. Unlike typical land hermit crabs, the coconut crab stops using a shell after the first year of life. This allows it to grow without being dependent on the availability of large shells. Very large coconut crabs may be more than forty years old and weigh more than 8 pounds (3.6 kilograms). As the name indicates, coconut is a favorite food. They also are known as robber crabs because of their habit of stealing objects and food to later test their edibility. I once was awakened in my tent by a coconut crab testing my big toe as it rested against a mosquito net. As could be expected, I awakened startled.

Although impressive, this species is not well suited for most people unless one can provide large enclosures. The general requirements of hermit crabs have to be met, but on a much larger scale. You need heat between 76°F–84°F (24°C–29°C) and relative humidity of 70 to 85 percent. You also need a fair amount of ground area with large-scale shelters and large water containers. On the rare occasions when I found coconut crabs during the day, they were inside tree hollows or in deep burrows. On a couple of occasions, I have also found coconut crabs clinging to the sides of a tree during the day in dark forests. At night, coconut crabs like climbing areas such as tree sections. In fact, they are remarkable climbers. I had one that tore open the bag I had it in and climbed straight up the edge of a partition to the ceiling of a hotel room. These crabs are active, very strong, and extremely talented escape artists. They will easily tear up wire mesh. They also need a deep substrate in which they can burrow during molting, allowing them to make 3 feet (91 cm) long and 1 to 2 feet (30–61 cm) deep molting burrows. Adults molt about once a year during the winter. They remain buried for more than a month during molting.

In general, coconut crabs have been short-lived in captivity and protocols for consistent long-term maintenance still have to be developed. Surprisingly few public aquaria and zoos have them on display. This is a very impressive species that deserves more research on captive rearing of young animals.

There are several other species of land hermit crabs, some of which are more colorful and attractive than the West Atlantic hermit crabs commonly sold. Considering the vagaries of the pet trade, it may well be that some of these exotic land hermit crabs could become available in the future. The general maintenance of most land hermit crabs will follow the basic pattern presented in this book.

Land Crabs

Recently, land crabs, usually members of the genus *Cardisoma* or *Gecarcinus*, have been offered in the pet trade and sometimes sold in kits consisting of an extra large plastic terrarium with sand and a small water dish. They will not survive long under such conditions. These large crabs require at least a 36-inch-long (91-cm) tank with 6 inches (15 cm) of sand as bottom substrate and another 6 to 12

Members of genus *Cardisoma* can require up to 1 ½ feet (45 cm) of substrate depth. These housing requirements have limited their survival rates in captive situations, as many novice crabbers may be unaware of these needs or unable to provide the proper conditions.

inches (15 to 30 cm) of moistened soil-sand mix on top. The bottom sand layer should be kept wet because land crabs need to burrow into the water-line when molting. Land crabs need heat, shelters, and high humidity. They are omnivorous, as are land hermit crabs. Land crabs need a shallow pan of water. They are recommended only for dedicated individuals willing to provide the space and conditions required.

RESOURCES

Burggren, W. W. and B. R. McMahon. 1988. *Biology of the Land Crabs.* London: Cambridge University Press.

Chace, F. A., Jr. and H. H. Hobbs, Jr. 1969. *The Freshwater and Terrestrial Decapod Crustaceans of the West Indies.* Washington, D.C.: Smithsonian Inst.

INDEX

substrates, 17–20, 50, 51–52; tank covers, 29; ventilation, 29; water containers, 18. *See also* humidity
humidity, 16, 17, 20, 27, 28–29, 46, 50. *See also* dehydration; misting; water husbandry. *See* maintenance
hygrometers, 28

I

illness. *See* diseases and disorders
ion concentration, 26–27, 28, 42

L

land crabs (*Cardisoma* and *Gecarcinus*), 51–52
landscaping, 17, 20
legs, 8, 37
lighting, 24
longevity, 5, 9, 50

M

maintenance: cleaning, 15, 18, 33–34; problems related to husbandry, 45–47
misting, 27, 33, 46
mites, 10, 47
molting: coconut crabs, 50; deaths, 12, 36–37; limb regeneration, 37; molt cycle, 5; preferred locations, 21; processes, 35–36; schedules, 37; substrates, 19, 20
mortality rates. *See* death
mouth, 8

O

overheating, 16, 24, 45

P

Pacific hermit crabs (*C. compressus*),13
parasites, 10, 47
personalities, 12–13
pinching, 14, 43
plants, 21

R

red-clawed freshwater crabs (*Sesarma bidens*), 49
regeneration of lost limbs, 37
reproduction, 8, 38–39

S

saltwater, 25, 26–27
scientific classification, 6
selecting crabs, 10–12
shells: changing, 9, 12, 39–40; cleaning, 40; fancy/painted, 40–41; lack of, 12, 42; water storage, 25, 27
shelters, 20–21
size: coconut crabs, 50; enclosures, 10–11, 15–16; West Atlantic land hermit crabs, 7, 9, 10–11
sleep patterns, 9
sound/noise (stridulation), 11, 42
strawberry hermit crabs (*C. perlatus*), 12, 13, 32
stress, 28
stridulation, 11, 42
substrates, 17–20, 25, 28–29, 50, 51–52

T

tail fan, 8
tannins, 31
taxonomy, 6
temperature: bathing water, 28; heating systems, 22–24; overheating, 16, 24, 45; range, 21–22, 50; thermometers, 23, 24; too cool, 22

U

urine, 34
UV lighting, 24

V

ventilation, 29

W

water, 18, 25–29, 33, 46. *See also* feeding; humidity
West Atlantic land hermit crab (*C. clypeatus*), 6, 39

ABOUT THE AUTHOR

Philippe de Vosjoli is the highly acclaimed author of the best-selling reptile care books, The Herpetocultural Library Series™. His work in the field of herpetoculture has been recognized nationally and internationally for establishing high standards for amphibian and reptile care. His books, articles, and other writings have been praised and recommended by numerous herpetological societies, veterinarians, and other experts in the field. Philippe de Vosjoli was also the cofounder and president of The American Federation of Herpetoculturists and was given the Josef Laszlo Memorial Award in 1995 for excellence in herpetoculture and his contribution to the advancement of the field.